About the Author

Judy R. Block is a freelance writer and editor. Besides editing and rewriting college texts, she has written legal self-help columns, business reports, and magazine articles on a variety of subjects.

Performance Appraisal on the Job:
Making It Work

Performance Appraisal on the Job: Making It Work

by Judy R. Block

A HANDS-ON MANAGEMENT GUIDE

EXECUTIVE ENTERPRISES PUBLICATIONS CO., INC.
33 WEST 60TH ST., NEW YORK, N.Y. 10023

PRENTICE-HALL, INC.
ENGLEWOOD CLIFFS, New Jersey 07632

ISBN 0-13-917386-52-3 {EXEC. ENT.}
ISBN 0-13-657080-1 {PRENTICE-HALL}
ISBN 0-13-657072-0 {PRENTICE-HALL, PBK}
Library of Congress Catalog Card No. 81-65122

INTRODUCTION
TO HANDS-ON
MANAGEMENT GUIDES

Performance Appraisal on the Job: Making It Work is the second in a new series published by Executive Enterprises Publications Co., Inc., and Prentice-Hall, Inc. Each book in the series digests the essence of the best, the most current, and the most practical ideas in management.

The stress of unexpected daily crises, the too often neglected long-term planning, the crush of personnel problems, the avalanche of memos, proposals, and minutes from meetings are only some of the nerve-racking pressures besieging managers today. A critical factor in these ever-mounting demands on the manager's time is the enormous amount of required reading. The material may be vital for the organization's welfare, or essential for the manager's career development, but who has the time? In one survey of 500 chief executives, 415, or 83 percent, said they lacked the time to keep up even with reading in their own field. How, then, can they find the time to read the piles of books offering the newest insights into management techniques?

This series is designed to meet that vital need for information to help managers do their best job of managing. Each book will:

- Describe a management process step by step;
- Alert managers to the most frequent and costly problems;
- Offer practical suggestions on how to solve the problems;
- Define key terms;
- Digest key theories and ideas;
- Narrate case illustrations of problems and solutions;
- List a bibliography of major publications on the subject.

Book #2 deals with performance appraisal on the job—potentially one of the most useful management tools, and certainly one of the most necessary, but unfortunately one of the most problem-ridden. The bibliography lists the books and articles from which this digest is drawn.

Myrna Lebov
Series Editor

CONTENTS

The author and publisher gratefully acknowledge the review and comments of R. Lawrence Ashe, Jr. Mr. Ashe is the Atlanta resident partner of the law firm of Paul, Hastings, Janofsky & Walker. He specializes in advice and litigation related to EEO and other personnel selection issues.

INTRODUCTION

APPRAISAL. The word makes us think of a valuable gem being scrutinized under a magnifying glass, a work of art being priced for auction, a houseful of furniture being inspected for an estate sale. In each instance, something is being valued—a price tag defines the worth.

When we evaluate employee performance, we normally do not place a dollar sign on our employees' worth. But we do scrutinize the pluses and minuses of their work, what the employee brings to the organization, and how he or she can bring even more.

Scrutinize. Judge. Predict. Counsel. Help. Train. These words sum up what performance appraisal is all about. By the time the performance appraisal process is over, we should be able to answer what management consultant George F. Truell sees as the two most important questions employees have about their work: How am I doing? Where am I going?

Phrased another way, these questions are also managerial concerns. To make decisions on raises, promotions, transfers, and discipline, we must know what employees have done in the past, how well they have done it, and how we can expect them to perform in the future either in the same job or in others.

These are what L. L. Cummings and Donald P. Schwab, authors of *Performance in Organizations: Determinants and Appraisals*, call the judgmental and counseling roles of performance appraisal. As we judge the past, we make administrative decisions: we decide how big a raise employees deserve, whether they are ready for a promotion or transfer, etc. As we look to the future, we try to help employees improve their performances. We involve ourselves and the employee, says the Conference Board, a nonprofit business research institution based in New York City, "in a problem-solving process that uses the experiences of the past to plan for better performance in the future."

When New York City's Mayor Ed Koch asks his constituents, "How am I doing?" he is asking for a performance review. The feedback he gets from the public tells him whether he measures up. Your employees, too, will welcome this kind of feedback if it is given in a constructive, sophisticated way. In talking to the employees in his firm, personnel expert Robert Finn discovered that most employees viewed their performance appraisal as an opportunity to talk things over with their supervisors in a way they had not been able to do throughout the year.

Then why the bad press? The respondents to a 1977 Conference Board study on managerial appraisal practices, which involved nearly three hundred firms of various sizes in a variety of industries, considered performance appraisal a necessary evil—something to be tolerated because it is impossible to manage an organization without it. From the problems management consultant and personnel expert Felix M. Lopez describes below, it is easy to see why performance appraisal systems sometimes fail:

- Managers don't like to "play God." They are uncomfortable talking about the employee's personality traits. Amateur psychiatry, in their opinion, has no place in the office.
- Managers don't want to embarrass their employees. If managers are not well trained, they may wind up presenting the evaluation information in an awkward, ill-conceived way.
- The results usually don't change anything. The manager who drifts through the appraisal without a well-thought-out plan will probably produce no permanent change in the employee's behavior.
- It takes a lot of time—too much, many managers believe. A thorough evaluation could take several hours. Add to that follow-up time and multiply both by the number of employees in the department and many managers feel overwhelmed by the task.
- William F. Glueck, author of *Foundations of Personnel*, adds the final point. Employees not given a top rating may give up trying—and their work shows it.

Despite these problems, performance appraisal systems have not been abandoned by industry. On the contrary, according to Truell, three out of four companies have some sort of formal evaluation plan.

The reason is clear. A well-planned, comprehensive performance appraisal system gives management the answers it needs. Performance appraisal systems received a resounding vote of confidence from the personnel executives who responded to the Conference Board study. Two out of three said that their system served their purposes. This figure rose to nine out of ten when the performance appraisal system had been developed within the preceding year.

Companies with no formal appraisal plan nevertheless evaluate their employees informally all the time. As managers size up their employees' work, as they decide who will do what over the coming months, as they listen to their employees' day-to-day problems, they are forming an opinion—an appraisal. "Appraisal is not an occasional, chance happening," says management expert Marion S. Kellogg. "It is basic to the manager's work and an essential part of his job."

But for an appraisal system to be effective, these intuitive, often haphazard reactions must be translated into a structured system. It is fair neither to managers nor employees nor organizations to base appraisals on poorly recollected events, hearsay, and personal likes and dislikes. Without a standard of measurement, which is applied to every employee's work, it is impossible to evaluate the past and plan for the future.

Appraising on the basis of gut feelings is simply bad business. But turned around—conducting appraisals on the basis of a formal, structured system—performance appraisals are an essential ingredient for business success.

PART 1: Setting the stage

If you are about to conduct a performance appraisal, stop! There is a lot of groundwork to cover first. That's our aim in this opening section. We'll give you the information you need to prepare yourself and your employees for the appraisal.

1. DEFINE THE JOB

Problem: No Definition

"I've had it," said Tom Pensky as he walked into Jenny Chamber's office. "I've been here over two months and I still don't know which way is up. No matter how hard I work, I never seem to catch up."

"Don't be so hard on yourself," said Jenny, Tom's co-worker. "It takes time to break into a new job. In a couple of weeks you'll have things under control."

"Not the way I'm going," said Tom. "I never know if I'm spending my time on the right work."

"Why don't you talk to your manager? He'll set your priorities straight."

"Take my word for it, I've tried. Mr. Parker says he wants to meet with me. But every time I call for an appointment, he's tied up with something urgent. The way I feel right now, by the time he gets to me, it'll be too late."

*   *   *   *   *

Step 1: Define the Job

Defining and clarifying your employees' job responsibilities is one of your key managerial roles. Unless your employees have precise definitions of their job functions, your performance appraisal system has little chance for success.

How to Define the Job

1. *Identify all the job's responsibilities right at the start.* Sit down with the employee and review the actual job analysis or meaningful position description for the job. If the employee still has questions, consider following George F. Truell's advice:

- First, work with your employee to develop a one-sentence "umbrella statement," which describes the job in general terms. The statement should clarify the special nature of the job, the employee's unique role in the company, and the role of the employee as a team member.
- Second, isolate the key responsibilities of the job—the performance elements crucial to the company's success. There are usually no more than five or six. Truell suggests that you assign each responsibility a segment of a circle—the more important the responsibility the larger the segment. This visual device will give employees a good idea of how they should spend their time.
- Third, list the most important subresponsibilities under each key responsibility. A word or phrase will do in each case.
- Finally, put these facts together on one sheet of paper. As Truell points out, the process of analyzing and defining the job is far more important than the ac-

tual list compiled. "Unless both parties have a clear understanding of the subordinate's job at the very beginning of the performance appraisal process," says Truell, "the whole system will break down."

2. *Review any major changes in job function as soon as they occur.* A promotion, demotion, or lateral move, an addition or shift of personnel, or even a new company policy can change a job description overnight. Meet with your employee as soon as changes occur and draw up a new list of job responsibilities.

3. *Set specific and mutually agreeable goals.* This look into the future will tell your employees where to concentrate their efforts and what results to aim for.

4. *Define an effective standard of performance for each job function.* This step tells employees what you expect of their work and what you consider a satisfactory performance. Try to base each standard on observable, quantifiable information. By telling the employee how much, how many, how well, and when, you are making your expectations clear. A due date of September 30 cannot be misunderstood and neither can a budget of $8,000 or an order for 500 new machines.

WARNING: Keep your surprises to a minimum if you want to maintain a sound appraisal system. Kellogg suggests a straightforward discussion with your employees as soon as they are hired. Tell them what judgments will be made and what standards of performance will be used.

2. OBSERVE. OBSERVE. OBSERVE.

Problem: Too Little Information

By the urgent tone of his supervisor's phone call, Bob Alexander, sporting goods manager at A and G Department Store, knew something was wrong.

"I expected Anna Wolf's performance appraisal two weeks ago," said Bob's supervisor, "and I can't wait any longer. I need a full report by the end of the week."

"You'll get it," answered Bob. His voice was filled with the confidence he knew his boss wanted to hear. But inside he felt a lot less sure of himself.

Swamped with work, Bob had put Anna Wolf's performance appraisal on the back burner—even though he knew months ago when her review was due. He had a sense that Anna, the head buyer in the sporting equipment department, was doing a good job, but he had nothing to base his impressions on. No hard facts.

"I'll keep an eye on her for a couple of days," thought Bob. "At least I'll have *some* idea of what she can do. And then I'll base the appraisal on whatever I see."

* * * * *

Step 2: Observe Performance Over a Period of Time

No matter what performance appraisal Anna Wolf received, she was shortchanged by Bob's failure to observe her work over a period of time. And so was the company. No one's work can be fairly appraised on the basis of a day's, a week's, or even a month's observation. It takes time—a lot of it—and a commitment to what R. Lawrence Ashe, Jr., an Atlanta attorney, terms understanding "both the duties of the job and the nature of the ratee's performance."

How to Make Well-Informed Observations

1. *Be completely familiar with the actual job analysis or position description before you start observing the employee's performance.* Start the observation process with a careful look at the job analysis and other personnel files that outline the scope of the job. There you will find information detailing the required standards of performance—the criteria against which to judge the employee's work.

A solid *job analysis* will give you the most information. According to the Uniform Guidelines on Employee Selection Procedures, this is "a detailed statement of work behaviors and other information relevant to the job." The job analysis sums up the important knowledge, skills, and functions that constitute effective job performance. If the file lacks this, look for the *job description*, which, according to the Uniform Guidelines, is "a general statement of job duties and responsibilities."

2. *Weed out the important job duties from the unimportant.* A construction foreman who appraises a carpenter's performance on the basis of how neatly he makes up his supply requests has missed the point. But you won't if you focus on the job's main objectives.

3. *Be sure your observations are balanced and fair.* Marion S. Kellogg points out that performance appraisal raters can easily err if they rely on "incidents that are either too old or too new" or if they base their judgments on an atypical work period. A glowing appraisal written ten years earlier, a negative review written immediately after the employee committed an uncharacteristic mistake, or a mixed review that failed to note an extraordinary amount of work pressure is neither balanced nor fair. Of course, as Ashe has pointed out in a phone conversa-

tion with the author, "ultimately it is the performance that counts no matter what the reason."

4. *Appraise only if you have enough information.* Almost inevitably, sometime in your career you, like Bob Alexander, will be pressed to complete a performance appraisal without sufficient information. Don't do it! General or vague impressions are not good enough. If you are forced into a corner by a performance appraisal deadline, tell your superior that you need more time. Otherwise, you will be unfair to the employee and the company. If you can't delay the appraisal, note on the appraisal form that your observations are insufficient to draw any conclusions about the employee's work.

5. *Always keep the appraisal's purpose in mind.* If you are appraising employees for a promotion, remember that the job skills needed on the new job may not be the same as those they are now using. Follow this general rule: always separate your comments about the employee's past performance from those concerning future potential. Since it is often impossible for you to know the exact requirements of a job for which the employee is being considered (the job may be in another department, for example), it is a good idea simply to list the employee's strengths and weaknesses and let the hiring supervisor make the judgment. Make your comments as specific and wide-ranging as possible.

WARNING: Assess job performance, not personality. When you dislike aspects of an employee's personality, it is all too easy to shift the focus of your observation from the individual's work to these personal characteristics. If you find yourself dwelling on such factors as stubbornness and a hot temper, take a different approach—at least for awhile. Focus on how well the employee does the job—the number of sales made, follow-through on assignments—and use this information as the basis of your review. You may find that the work problems *are* rooted in the employee's personality. But let your observations prove this to you. Don't assume it from the start.

3. MAKE A DECISION

Problem: The Confused Manager

Joyce Stone, account supervisor at the ABC advertising agency, leafed through Jeff Cunningham's report as she spoke to him on the phone. "You need a lot more detail in this presentation, Jeff, before I can offer it to the clients. You know how clients are these days. Before they spend a dollar of their advertising budget, they want everything spelled out. Please revise it and get back to me tomorrow."

As Joyce Stone hung up the phone, she felt confused about Jeff's work. Maybe she was being too hard on him. Maybe her demands were unreasonable and his work was really okay. Joyce knew she had to decide very quickly how she felt about Jeff's work; his performance appraisal was due next month. The trouble was she just didn't know how she would ever make up her mind.

*　　*　　*　　*　　*

Step 3: Make a Decision

Joyce Stone found out something that almost all managers learn: when you have mixed feelings about an employee's work, your doubts can affect your ability to conduct an effective performance appraisal. When this happens, turn to the facts and let them guide your opinion. (For common performance appraisal pitfalls, see pp. 32 and 45.)

How to Translate Your Observations Into Decisions

1. *Aim for accuracy*. After you have observed the employee for a period of time (how long depends on the needs of the employee and the demands of the job), decide how you feel about the individual's work. Then think about your decision for a day or two to be sure you are being honest with yourself.

As Ashe points out, managers often have a problem giving employees the rating they deserve. "While overzealous rigor is an occasional problem," says Ashe, "excessive leniency is the rule rather than the exception." Ashe attributes this tendency to several factors:

- an unwillingness to confront the employee;
- a hope that the employee's performance will improve and equal the performance rating (wishful thinking);
- a desire to justify a raise or promotion (the manager keeps out of hot water);
- a fear that the employee will claim an infringement of the equal employment opportunity laws (bending over backwards to be fair or at least avoid a hassle); and
- sheer ignorance or carelessness (attitudinal problems that can be difficult to solve).

If you have trouble giving employees the appraisal they deserve, remember that excessive leniency can backfire. Sometime in the future, you will have to deal with employee expectations—a raise, a promotion—which you will be unable to meet. In addition, if the employee's work deteriorates even further, you may be faced with the unenviable job of firing the individual after having given a good performance review. You also will make your job of improving the employee's performance even harder, since the employee thinks he or she is doing just fine now.

Lester R. Bittel, author of *What Every Supervisor Should Know*, suggests one way to be sure of accurate evaluations: check for a variation of appraisals. "In any group," says Bittel, "there should be a variety of performances." He estimates that three-quarters of the employees will be in the middle ratings (fair to good); one-eighth will be rated at the top (very good to exceptional); and another eighth will be at the bottom (fair to unsatisfactory).

2. *Guard against improper bias.* Studies have shown that how you feel about your employees' sex, race, or age may influence the way you rate them. Your biases may cause you to appraise your employees either lower or higher than they deserve. People who have antifemale bias, for example, are likely to give women a low rating regardless of their performances. But as William J. Bigoness points out in the *Journal of Applied Psychology*, high-performing females are often rated significantly higher than high-performing males.

Gary Dessler, author of *Management Fundamentals: A Framework*, takes a philosophic view of this confusion. "There is no easy way to predict just what effect this 'bias' problem may have on an appraisal," says Dessler. "About the best you can do is be on guard against being a 'biased' appraiser."

Learning the Art of Criticism

"Telling employees they don't measure up is one of the hardest things for most managers to do," says Dorothy Lester, personnel manager of a medium-sized public relations firm in New York City. "Managers don't know how to criticize, discipline, or warn their employees, with the result that most performance appraisals aren't worth the paper they're written on."

According to Lester, managers can't expect to learn how to criticize at performance appraisal time. "This kind of trial by fire," says Lester, "simply doesn't work." Lester suggests instead that managers follow this step-by-step approach to mastering the art of criticism:

1. *Constructively criticize new employees as soon as they start their jobs.* Don't wait for appraisal time. Tell the employee when you spot a problem. Try to be constructive and helpful.

2. *Find out what caused the problem.* Did the employee misunderstand his or her job responsibilities? Was a careless error or a simple case of forgetfulness involved?

3. *Document your conversation.* Send a memo to the employee and place one in the personnel file. When you put your criticism in writing, says Lester, there is no possibility of confusion.

4. *Immediately confront the employee the next time the problem arises.* This time delve a little deeper into the cause of the problem. Try to find out if the employee is having trouble with one particular job responsibility, a large part of the job, or the whole job. When possible, develop an improvement plan. If the whole job is going wrong, don't mince words. You're not doing the employee, the company, or yourself any favors.

5. *Document your conversation and recommendations.* Your written comments may prove invaluable later on if you have to dismiss the employee for unsatisfactory performance.

Lester is convinced that these informal performance appraisals will strengthen your ability to honestly criticize your employees' work. "Each experience," says Lester, "makes the next one easier. By the time you have to complete the formal performance review, you'll be ready."

WARNING: If you use someone else's opinion in the appraisal, be sure you know how that person arrived at it and what standards were used. Kellogg warns against relying on another manager's performance appraisal if the manager's comments are simply general statements. According to Kellogg, these statements will mean little if you do not know the specific details of the employee's work. So, get these details from your colleagues.

PART 2: Following the script

The stage is set. You have the information you need to conduct the performance appraisal. What next? If your organization already has a formal performance appraisal system, you must now learn the specifics of the policy.

However, if your organization does not yet have such a system, you can use the information in this section to persuade your personnel executives to introduce one and, perhaps, to help write the script. Or, if your company's evaluation system needs revision, you may be able to help rewrite the script.

If introduction or revision of a system is on the agenda, your organization must first make sure that it chooses the right appraisers and an effective time schedule. Next comes devising the system itself.

4. CHOOSE THE RIGHT APPRAISER

Problem: Somebody Has to Do It

Rachel Kane held a copy of her company's performance appraisal form in her hand when Arnold O'Neil walked into her office.

"Where's Amy Anderson's appraisal?" asked Rachel, gesturing to Arnold with the report. "I need one of these right away."

"I know you do and believe me I haven't been avoiding the work. I just want to be sure that nothing will go wrong."

"What do you mean?" asked Rachel.

"I've been watching Amy for a long time," said Arnold, "and her work has problems—serious ones. She also has a temper. She almost bit my head off last week when I made a small comment about her work."

"So?"

"Well," Arnold said slowly, "I don't think I'm the right person to handle this appraisal. Amy might be more receptive to a committee report."

"We're not going to change our system to handle this one case," said Rachel. "You'll have to deal with it."

"I'll do my best," said Arnold as he turned to leave Rachel's office. His stomach churned when he realized he would have to face Amy alone in the morning.

*   *   *   *   *

Step 4: Choose the Right Appraiser

When employees receive poor performance reviews, no one wants to be the one to tell them. When they receive favorable reviews, telling them can still be difficult and time-consuming. Nevertheless, performance appraisals must be made and someone has to make them. That person is usually the employee's immediate supervisor, but there are options.

How to Choose the Appraiser

1. *Examine the options carefully.* Each has its pros and cons, so determine which will meet your company's needs. Here are the choices:

- *Supervisor evaluation.* According to Cummings and Schwab, having an employee's immediate supervisor conduct the appraisal makes good business sense. It is the supervisor's "duty and obligation," say the authors, to pass judgment on employees' work and to try to help them improve. Since managers are in the best position to observe their employees' performances and since they generally significantly influence the size and frequency of raises and promotions, they can do this more easily than anyone else.

- *Peer evaluation.* Having co-workers appraise a fellow employee's work prevents some of the problems inherent in a one-person appraisal system. A peer evaluation does not fall apart if one person lacks the skill to conduct a fair and effective appraisal. And, as Arnold O'Neil suspected, it is a lot easier to share the burden of "playing God" than to shoulder it alone.

According to Cummings and Schwab, peer evaluations can work only if certain conditions are met. First, the employees must trust each other, have a sense of sharing, and above all not be in competition for raises. Second, they must be completely familiar with the employee's work—what work is done and how well. When these conditions are met, says Dessler, peer evaluation is effective "in predicting future management success."

- *Rating committees*. These committees are usually made up of an employee's immediate supervisor and three or four other supervisors who know the employee's work. Using a committee, says Dessler, helps to avert some of the serious problems like bias and the halo effect (see pp. 45, 53) that can crop up when one person does the job. And committees compensate for the fact that a single supervisor cannot observe everything an employee does; it takes several people in different managerial roles to evaluate the employee as a whole.

- *Self-appraisals*. In one sense, self-appraisal is inevitable. When employees walk into an appraisal interview with their supervisor, they almost always have a sense of how they have performed; and a good part of the interview is spent reacting to that.

As Dessler points out, this method has had mixed success. It can work in a developmental appraisal connected with a Management by Objectives Program. Here, goals of personal growth, self-motivation, and organizational potential are set by employees working with their managers. Self-appraisal is then used by employees to evaluate how close they actually come to meeting their goals. But studies have shown that self-appraisals are not always accurate. "In general," say Cummings and

Schwab, "subordinates tend to evaluate their performance more favorably than do their superiors." Self-appraisals can be valuable evaluation tools if they are used to counsel and develop an employee but not to make salary and promotion decisions.

2. *To avoid bias and any infringement of the equal employment opportunity laws, submit each appraisal to at least one other reviewer.* It is a good idea to have someone else in authority review and sign the appraisal. If possible, this should be a person familiar with the employee's work—usually the first reviewer's immediate supervisor.

According to the Conference Board, companies use this secondary review to "monitor and control" the appraisal process. The appraisal and recommendations for raises and promotions are more likely to be fair and accurate if they are reviewed at a higher level of management.

The person reviewing the appraisal should sign or initial the form after reading it. (This does not necessarily mean that the reviewer agrees with your judgments although a consensus is desirable and usually obtainable.) The best time to do this, says the Conference Board, is before you meet with the employee. A prior review is critical if you plan to talk to the employee about money.

WARNING: Conducting the appraisal without clear written instructions from your superior or a formal training period can lead to problems. No matter how carefully your company's appraisal program is structured, it will be useless to you if you have not received the proper orientation.

5. DECIDE ON A TIME SCHEDULE

Problem: Procrastination

"I have all my appraisals under control," said George Mason, production manager for a medium-sized ice cream manufacturer, to his colleague Fred Owen. "I've been keeping a close eye on my staff and I know exactly how they're doing."

"But just last week you told me that none of your appraisals was done?" Fred looked confused.

"Well, I haven't completed any of the paperwork or met with any of my people—but I could do that in my sleep."

"When are you putting everything together?" asked Fred. "I evaluate my people every six months."

"When the time is right," answered George. "That'll probably be when Mr. Becker starts to hound me."

*   *   *   *   *

Step 5. Decide on an Appraisal Time Schedule

George Mason may have had all his performance appraisal information on hand, but it was useless to his employees and to the company. An appraisal system can work only if evaluations are conducted at regular intervals. If used haphazardly or at the manager's discretion, it will fall apart.

How to Set Up a Performance Appraisal Time Schedule

1. *Determine how frequently your employees would benefit from a performance review.* Analyze whether your employees would benefit most from a frequent review schedule (every three months, for example), a once-a-year review, or evaluations timed to major projects throughout the year.

According to Glueck, the vast majority of appraisals are given annually. Studies have shown that 74 percent of white-collar and 58 percent of blue-collar employees receive an annual performance review; 25 percent of white-collar and 30 percent of blue-collar employees are evaluated semiannually, and about 10 percent are evaluated more often than semiannually.

If you decide on an annual review, you can schedule it either on the individual's employment anniversary or during a set period when all the organization's performance appraisals are done.

Even though yearly reviews may be the most convenient, psychologists say they may not produce the desired results. If your aim is to correct employee performance, studies have shown that the more often you review an employee's work the better—especially when your comments are connected to an action that just occurred. "More meaningful and timely feedback of performance data is achieved," say personnel specialists responding to the Conference Board study, "by reviewing performance whenever significant projects or tasks are completed." The information is fresher in both the manager's and employee's minds.

2. *Weigh your own needs.* If you have, say, twenty employees in your department and you evaluate them after every major project, you won't have time for other work.

What's the solution? Compromise! One way is to *informally* appraise your employees as frequently as possible and then *formally* summarize their performances at evaluation time. Base your informal appraisals on adequate information and try to keep your personal feelings out of the picture.

3. *Consider establishing a variable-interval performance schedule.* If you don't feel overwhelmed by the task of evaluating your employees whenever they need it, set up a variable-interval performance schedule. Cummings and Schwab suggest four ways to do this:

- Tie your evaluation to the completion of a major project.
- If this is impossible, work out with the employee the best time to review a project in progress.
- Leave the appraisal scheduling up to the employee. Only competent employees who have little contact with their managers should be given this option. A field sales representative, for example, would benefit from this kind of scheduling.
- Make the decision on your own. This method, however, encourages managers to review only effective performers: it's easier to postpone giving someone a bad review than to give it.

WARNING: If you appraise a group of employees at about the same time, don't let your feelings about one employee affect your appraisal of the others. Cummings and Schwab point out the danger of giving an artificially high rating to an average employee who happens to follow a weak employee and a low rating to someone whose appraisal follows an outstanding worker's. This *contrast effect* can make even the best prepared appraisal hard to defend.

Variable-interval scheduling can mitigate this problem. It allows you to avoid evaluating several people at one time, and it also can ensure that the order of appraisals will change from year to year.

6. USE AN APPRAISAL SCALE

Problem: Fitting the Pieces Together

"It looks like someone just dropped a ton of paper on your desk," said Ann Milton as she walked into Betty Swerdling's office. "No one would let me get by with that mess at my company." Ann was a product manager at a nearby company. She and Betty were in the same carpool and often met at Betty's office at the end of the day.

"It's no joke," said Betty. "I have to put all this together for a performance review. I don't know where to begin."

"What do all these papers say?" asked Ann.

"I've spent months observing an employee's work and I took notes on everything. The trouble is I don't know how to organize what I have."

"Working with my company's evaluation scale usually helps me out of this kind of mess," said Ann. "Which one are you using?"

"Well ... I never bothered to learn much about our appraisal scale," admitted Betty.

"Maybe that's your problem."

* * * * *

Step 6: Use a Performance Appraisal Scale

The appraisal scale is a valuable tool for organizing and evaluating the reams of information that are part of every performance appraisal. As Betty Swerdling learned the hard way, conducting performance appraisals without an appraisal scale unnecessarily complicates the procedure.

If your organization already uses a performance appraisal scale, go over the instructions carefully. Try to learn as much as possible about the appraisal process so that you are fully prepared the first time. If your organization does not use an appraisal scale, the information in this section will help you select a scale best suited to your company's needs.

How to Select a Performance Appraisal Scale

1. *Choose a scale that is reliable and valid.* According to the Conference Board, these two criteria are essential characteristics of a good appraisal system. Your company's performance scale should aim for *reliability*—a system that yields consistent data—and *validity*—a system that deals with relevant employee performance.

2. *Be sure the system is carefully structured to make the evaluations as objective as possible.* The scale helps provide the structure.

3. *Work with an easily understood, job-related performance appraisal form.* The form your company chooses should clearly state the major duties to be measured. It should tie job performance to specific observable evidence. Ashe suggests that you avoid appraising abstract traits and lean instead toward specific, observable conduct. He also stresses manager input in the development of appraisal forms; no one knows better than you the behaviors that should be measured.

4. *Have your personnel department review the appraisal to be sure it is consistent with others used in the organization.* Since appraisal documents compare employees in different units of the

organization, it is critical to use standardized forms and methods of administration. According to the Conference Board, a nonstandardized system "raises the probability that at least some differences in the performance measure of different employees are in fact the result of the appraisal system and its administration rather than of real differences in employee performance."

5. *Understand the options for an appraisal scale.* If your organization is now starting an appraisal system or revising an old one, your knowledge of these options can make you a valuable asset. The main ones are described below.

Some methods compare one employee's work to another's. These are classified into two groups: *ranking procedures* and *forced distribution*. Ranking procedures include the following methods:

- *Straight ranking.* One of the simplest performance appraisal methods, straight ranking compares one employee's work to another's. You are asked to choose the best performer, the second best, and so on, until you reach the employee you consider least effective.

- *Alternate ranking.* This popular and simple rating method involves ranking your employees from best to worst on a particular work characteristic. To do this, first list all your employees and then cross out the names of those whose work you don't know. Then choose the employee who rates highest on a particular characteristic and the one who rates lowest. Alternating between highest and lowest, choose the next highest and the next lowest until all the employees have been rated.

- *Paired Comparison.* In this variation of straight ranking, you pair, and compare, each employee with all others on the trait being ranked. To do this, make a list of all possible employee pairs. In a four-person department, for example, employee A would be compared with B, A with C, A with D, B with C, and so on. Then for each trait, analyze who is the most effective employee of the pair. After all the traits are compared, add up the number of times the employee was rated highest. The employee chosen most often for traits of equal value receives the highest rating.

The forced distribution method may bring back memories of college exams because it is similar to grading on a curve. As its name suggests, you are forced to place a predetermined percentage of employees in various performance categories for each characteristic you rate. You may choose, for example, to rate 10 percent of your employees in the highest performance category, 20 percent in the next highest, 40 percent in the mid-performance range, 20 percent below average, and 10 percent in the lowest category. Dessler suggests you do this by writing each employee's name on a separate card. As you appraise each trait, place the employee's card in the appropriate category.

Forced distribution is a less rigorous and more easily performed method of performance appraisal than ranking. As Ashe points out, "it avoids pretending a fineness of judgment that doesn't exist in fact." Instead of ranking employees one by one from the highest to the lowest, forced distribution allows you to group employees in broad performance categories. This is especially useful in a large department where it is often difficult to rate an employee as best, second best, third best, and so on.

Other appraisal methods are based on absolute standards: the employee is evaluated against written job criteria rather than against other employees. These methods can be either qualitative or quantitative. *Qualitative methods* determine whether the employee possesses some job-related characteristic. These methods, which seek yes or no answers, include the following performance scales:

- *Critical incident method.* In this technique, managers who are familiar with the requirements of a job prepare a list of the most and least effective employee behaviors. These *critical incidents* are then combined into a small number of behavioral categories. Out of 100 critical incidents, for example, W. K. Kircher and Marvin Dunnette, writing in the journal *Personnel*, wound up with thirteen behavioral categories to evaluate salespeople. Their categories included such essential activities as initiating sales contacts and calling on accounts.

Using these behavioral categories, managers can appraise their employees' typical behaviors throughout the year. By keeping a log of good and bad behaviors in each category, you can base your evaluations on a record of specific incidents. This helps avoid the tendency of basing your evaluation on the most recent incidents.

- *Weighted checklist.* This method is similar to the critical incident method. First, descriptive statements about effective and ineffective job behaviors are developed by a group of managers and personnel specialists. Then these statements are sorted into piles according to how favorable or unfavorable they are for successful performance; assigned scores, with low scores representing unfavorable behavior and high scores representing favorable behavior; and weighted according to the average score.

  A manager who must appraise an employee is given a copy of these statements—but no ratings are included next to the items. The manager is asked to check off those traits the employee has displayed. By summing up the scores of the items that have been checked (the manager is given these scores after the evaluation is complete), the manager can determine the employee's evaluation.

- *Forced choice methods.* In this appraisal method, statements about job performance are obtained from managers and personnel specialists familiar with the job. These statements are judged according to their ability to differentiate between successful and unsuccessful performance (referred to as the discrimination index) and their desirability—whether they are favorable or unfavorable statements to make about an employee's behavior. These statements are then grouped into two-, three-, or four-item clusters that make it more difficult for the evaluator to judge which statements apply to the most effective employees. The evaluator is asked to check the one item in the cluster that best describes the employee. Then the administrators of the appraisal system use the discrimination index of the items checked to score the employee and come up with a performance appraisal.

Unlike qualitative methods of performance appraisal, *quantitative methods* measure *how much* of a certain job characteristic the employee possesses. These methods include the following performance appraisal tools.

- *Conventional ratings.* According to Cummings and Schwab, conventional ratings are the most popular appraisal form. This method attempts to measure employee behavior along a continuous scale. The manager judges the degree to which the employee exhibits the behavior, assigning a value along the scale. In most cases, the manager can choose from among five, seven, or nine value points along the scale.
- *Behaviorally anchored rating scales (BARS).* A relatively new development in the appraisal field, BARS are generally developed in five steps:

  1. Critical incidents—examples of effective and ineffective behavior—are isolated by managers and personnel specialists familiar with the job.

2. Performance dimensions are developed—the critical incidents are combined into a smaller set of performance dimensions, which are then defined.
3. Incidents are reallocated. A second group of managers and personnel specialists are given the clusters and critical incidents and asked to reassign each incident to the cluster that best describes it. When at least 50 percent of the second group agrees with the original cluster choice, the critical incident becomes a permanent part of the evaluation scale.
4. The incidents are scaled. The second managerial group uses a seven- to nine-point scale to describe how effectively or ineffectively the behavior described in the incident represents performance.
5. The final instrument is developed. Six or seven incidents are included in each cluster. These incidents "anchor" statistically determined points along the rating scale. They help the manager specify behavior that is extremely good, slightly good, poor, and so on.

Even though BARS are time-consuming to develop, they provide clearer standards than other methods, a precise gauge of performance, feedback opportunities, and a clarity of job dimensions.

In addition to these methods, Management by Objectives (MBO) can be used as an appraisal tool. In this method, the employee and the manager set work objectives that are as quantifiable as possible—how many sales are made, clients contacted, and so on. Employees are given a time period to achieve their objectives; their efforts are then evaluated against these objectives. Managers gauge whether employees reached their goals and if not, what part they completed. Using this information as a guide, employees set new goals for the next appraisal period.

According to Cummings and Schwab, because MBO relies on the employee's own objectives, it limits itself to managerial and professional personnel who can develop their jobs according to their own interests and capabilities.

WARNING: If you are in the position to help choose a new appraisal scale for your organization, be sure to select the scale best suited to your employees' needs rather than trying to fit your employees' needs into the requirements of a scale.

---

7. WORK WITH
THE WRITTEN APPRAISAL

Problem: Unfinished Business

"You look pleased with yourself," said Kevin Blake as he walked into Charles Armon's office.

"Well, I should be," answered Charles. "I finally know how to use the company's performance appraisal scale. It took a lot of work, but it was worth it."

"How are you planning to handle employees who want to review their appraisals?" asked Kevin. "And have you thought about what you'll say if an employee decides to appeal?"

Charles looked puzzled. "You mean I have to worry about these things now? I thought learning the scale was enough."

*　　*　　*　　*　　*

Step 7: Learn How to Work With the Written Appraisal

Choosing and learning the performance appraisal scale is only half the job. You must also know how to put your evaluations on paper and how to handle the written appraisal with regard to company policy and employee demands.

How to Work With Written Performance Appraisals

1. *Present as opinion any appraisal about the future*. When speculation about an employee's future with the company creeps into the appraisal process, be careful to present your statements as subjective opinion. According to Kellogg, if you make the mistake of "playing God"—of predicting what will happen two, three, or even ten years down the road—you will place the employee at an unfair advantage.

2. *Make written appraisals consistent with oral ones*. Everyone agrees it is difficult and unpleasant to tell employees face to face that they are not doing well, but it must be done. You are cheating yourself, your employees, and the organization if you gloss over their poor performances in the appraisal interview but include this information in the appraisal file. Moreover, you may be opening yourself up to equal employment opportunity complaints.

3. *Decide how long you will keep the appraisal forms*. According to the Conference Board survey, 99 percent of the firms it studied maintained performance appraisal files. These files may be kept for one, two, or more years. The length of time is up to you—as long as you are *consistent* in your policy. Kellogg suggests that you "keep all appraisals or destroy all those over a certain age or keep the last one for each job held."

4. *Let employees review their written appraisals*. Give employees the opportunity to see what you have written on their appraisal forms. It shows that you have been forthright with them in your oral comments.

5. *Allow employees to submit written comments on their appraisals*. Give them the opportunity to include both their positive and negative views in the appraisal file.

6. *Give employees the opportunity to agree or disagree with the listing of major duties on which their performances were rated*. You can include their comments in the appraisal file.

7. *Have your employees sign their appraisals*. Their signatures mean only that they have read the review, not necessarily that they agree with it.

8. *Give employees the right to appeal*. The appeal process is a safeguard against unfairness or inaccuracy. And as Ashe points out, it also "increases the appearance of basic due process."

9. *Don't abuse the privacy of the performance appraisal*. What you say to the employee during the performance appraisal interview and what you write in the performance appraisal form are between you, the employee, and those who are entitled to the information. If a third party asks you for appraisal information, Kellogg suggests that you first find out the reason for the inquiry. Then you can decide which details to provide. Be sure to tell the employee about the inquiry.

WARNING: In the near future, you may be required to open your performance appraisal files to employee inspection. In 1974, Congress passed the Federal Privacy Act to "provide certain safeguards for an individual against an invasion of personal privacy." These safeguards include a limit on the amount of information in federal agency files. Recently, attempts have been made to extend the law to state and local governments and to the private sector.

In California, employees already have the right to examine their personnel files for data on employment qualifications, pay raises, promotions and transfers, and terminations.

8. LET THE FACTS GUIDE YOUR APPRAISAL

Problem: A Partial Truth

"How could you have done this to me, Ed?" asked Jim Ryan. "When I took your advice and promoted Jerry Bowen to chief accounting clerk, I thought he could handle the *whole* job. Now I find out that he's a whiz at payroll control but a loser at almost everything else."

"I'm sorry, Jim," said Ed. "But Jerry was a top performer in my office. He turned around our payroll system on his own."

"But what about the rest of his work?"

"Well, come to think of it, there were problems in . . ."

"See?" interrupted Jim. "You misled me about Jerry's qualifications. I guess pawning him off on me was an easy way to get rid of him."

"But I didn't," insisted Ed. "I thought all his work was good."

"Try that line on someone else," fumed Jim as he stormed out of the room.

* * * * *

Step 8: Let the Facts Guide Your Appraisal

Ed was guilty of one of the most common performance appraisal errors. He fell victim to the *halo effect*. He let his overall impression of Jerry Bowen's performance cloud his appraisal of the employee's specific skills.

How to Overcome Performance Appraisal Pitfalls

1. *Beware of the halo effect.* It's all too easy to generalize about an employee's performance—to allow your reaction to one quality color your entire opinion of the employee's work. To avoid this, Bittel suggests that you deal with each rating factor separately. Rate all your employees on one factor before moving on to the next.

2. *Avoid central tendency mistakes.* Central tendency prob lems occur when managers rate all their employees in the high average range. No distinction is made among employees doing outstanding, above average, below average, or unacceptable work. To avoid this problem, consider using the forced distribution appraisal method, which forces you to place a predetermined number of employees in each rating category (see p. 36).

3. *Guard against being too lenient.* The central tendency problem points out how difficult it is for many managers to be totally honest in their evaluations. If you find yourself leaning over backwards to give an employee a good rating, remember that you are undercutting the performances of the superior employees.

4. *Don't expect the impossible.* Imposing superhuman performance standards on your employees will create tension and discontent. If you find that no one's work pleases you, reevaluate your attitudes. Try to discover if your standards are excessively harsh. As Bittel says, "It's no pleasure to work for a supervisor who takes good performance for granted."

5. *Keep bias out of the performance appraisal.* Bias is one of the problems that can't be swept under the rug in the hope it will go away. Managers inevitably bring their personal feelings into the appraisal situation, and these feelings often get in the way of an objective review. As you will see in the next chapter, discrimination against any group or individual on the basis of race, color, sex, religion, national origin, handicap, or age is illegal, and increasing pressure is being exerted on managers to safeguard the principle of equal opportunity for all.

WARNING: Bias can take another form. When you base your appraisal only on those events that occurred in the recent past, you ignore the major part of your employee's job history. According to Glueck, you can lessen this problem by using such appraisal techniques as the critical incident method and management by objectives and by scheduling your evaluations at fairly frequent intervals.

---

9. COMPLY WITH EEO REQUIREMENTS

Problem: Keeping Up With the Judges

Mary Jenkins hurried into Bob Brown's office waving a report in her hand. "Have you seen this?" asked Mary. "There's just been another EEO court decision affecting performance appraisals. We'd better study this ruling before next month's appraisal period or we'll both be in hot water."

Bob Brown sat back in his chair as he skimmed the pages of the report. When he finished, he looked up at Mary and smiled. "I don't know what you're worried about," said Bob. "This is just a lot of legal hogwash."

"How can you say that?" interrupted Mary. "If that court decision stands we'll have to scrap a good part of our appraisal system."

"Not if I have anything to do with it," snapped Bob. "We've used the same system for years and we're not going to change now. It works—no matter what the court says."

"But we're not meeting the EEO guidelines. Look . . . right here . . . it says the appraisal system must be . . . ."

"I don't care what it says," said Bob. "We're not going to change."

*   *   *   *   *

47

Step 9: Comply With EEO Requirements

In these times of strict equal employment opportunity (EEO) guidelines concerning performance appraisals and court cases testing the legality of existing systems, Bob Brown's attitude is short-sighted—and may prove costly. To understand why, we will take a look at what the EEO laws say about performance appraisals and how court cases have affected EEO policy.

What the Law Says

Between 1963 and 1974, Congress passed four laws to protect workers from discrimination on the job:

- The Equal Pay Act of 1963 sets down the equal pay for equal work doctrine.
- Title VII of the Civil Rights Act of 1964, the most inclusive equal employment opportunity law, prohibits discrimination on the basis of sex, religion, race, color, or national origin. It was amended in 1972 and again in 1978.
- The Age Discrimination in Employment Act of 1967, amended in 1974 and again in 1978, bars discrimination against job applicants and employees aged forty to seventy. (Federal employees are not subject to an upper age limit.)
- The Rehabilitation Act of 1973, amended in 1974 and again in 1978, requires companies with government contracts of $2,500 or more to take steps to reasonably accommodate the physical and mental needs of handicapped employees and applicants.
- The Vietnam Era Veterans' Readjustment Assistance Act of 1972, reenacted in 1974 as the Vietnam Era Veterans' Readjustment Act, and further amended in 1976 and again in 1978, requires companies with

government contracts of $10,000 or more to take affirmative action to employ and advance in employment qualified disabled veterans and veterans of the Vietnam era.

In addition, Executive Order 11246 requires all companies doing more than $10,000 worth of business with the federal government and all construction projects that have received even partial federal funding to have nondiscrimination clauses in their contracts. Contractors with more than fifty employees and contracts of $50,000 or more must submit written affirmative action programs.

The Equal Employment Opportunity Commission (EEOC), with the major responsibility for administering these laws, sets down specific guidelines employers must meet. (The Rehabilitation Act, the Vietnam Era Veterans Act, and Executive Order 11246 are enforced by the Office of Federal Contract Compliance Programs, U.S. Department of Labor.) Since performance appraisals are used, in part, to determine pay increases, promotions, transfers, and training opportunities for protected classes of workers, they are EEOC concerns.

To clarify the exact requirements that appraisal and other selection systems must meet, in 1978 the EEOC, working with several other federal agencies, put together the Uniform Guidelines on Employee Selection Procedures, which included the following points:

- To continue using an appraisal system that has adversely affected one or more protected groups, the company must demonstrate that the system is "valid," that it is job-related, and that it accurately measures significant aspects of job performance.
- The company must establish that there is no other available method for achieving the same necessary business purpose that would be less discriminatory in its effects, and none can be developed. According to the courts, the plaintiff rather than the defendant must demonstrate the availability of the alternatives.

According to the 1977 Conference Board study on appraising managerial performance, few companies have attempted to validate their appraisal systems. And, the Conference Board goes on to state, "as a practical matter, it would be almost impossible to establish the validity of many appraisal systems used today." Instead of relying on hard, objective evidence related to the central purpose of the job, companies have traditionally based their appraisal systems on such subjective criteria as relationships with people, appearance, capacity for growth, and loyalty to the organization.

What the Courts Have Said

These EEO principles have been extended and reinforced in court cases. Here are some of the most important decisions:

- *Griggs v. Duke Power Co.* (1971). To gather what it considered objective evidence for hiring, promotion, and so on, the Duke Power Company of North Carolina required employees to have a high school or equivalency diploma and a passing score on a written test. Duke's black employees promptly sued. They charged that this kind of "objective" system would close blacks out of the higher-paying jobs since three times as many whites as blacks in North Carolina received high school diplomas. In its ruling for the black employees, the United States Supreme Court said: "Practices, procedures or tests, neutral on their face and even neutral in terms of intent cannot be maintained if they operate to 'freeze' the status quo of prior discriminatory employment practices." The Court went on to say that objective tests of this kind must be job-related.

- *Albemarle Paper Co. v. Moody* (1975). Albemarle Paper Company, another North Carolina employer, used preemployment written tests to measure reading and general intelligence. Blacks, whose failure rate was much higher than that of whites, charged that the tests were discriminatory.

  To test the validity of their system and show a correlation between test scores and employee performance, Albemarle hired an industrial psychologist and a university's statistical service. By comparing supervisors' judgments of job performance with test scores, the experts concluded that the test was job-related and its use complied with EEOC guidelines.

  The Supreme Court disagreed. The Court cited Albemarle's reliance on subjective and unstructured supervisory appraisals of job performance as the major problem. By basing their appraisals on vague standards whose job-relatedness was questionable, Albemarle failed to meet the EEOC requirement for objective evidence.

- *Rowe v. General Motors* (1972). The Fifth Circuit Court of Appeals found that General Motor's all-white management force could not on the face of it be expected to fairly evaluate the performances of blacks and other minority groups. This decision has far-reaching implications. Companies whose appraisal systems are run by middle-aged white males may be asked to validate their systems and prove that their appraisals are not indirectly contributing to discriminatory employment practices.

These and other cases form the environment in which companies operate their appraisal systems. Complying with the law in the design and implementation of appraisal systems is one of the overriding challenges facing managers in the 1980s.

How to Comply With EEOC Requirements

The EEOC and three other federal agencies have told employers what they *cannot* do, but they have not provided *definitive* guidelines for solving the performance appraisal puzzle. We must piece these together ourselves from the agencies' various pronouncements and come up with a plan of action that has the best chance of succeeding, says *EEO Today* in an Autumn 1980 article entitled "Reducing the EEO Risks in Performance Appraisals." Here are the guidelines *EEO Today* suggests:

1. *Base your appraisal on a comprehensive job analysis.* EEOC guidelines dictate that you measure job performance against specific, clearly defined standards of performance. The performance you appraise, says the EEOC, "must represent major critical work behaviors as revealed by a careful job analysis." Without a clear, written statement of job responsibilities, you increase your risk of EEO liability.

2. *Know the details of your company's nondiscriminatory policies.* You and every other manager in the company should aim for the uniform application of all appraisal guidelines.

3. *Avoid subjective criteria.* According to the *Albemarle Paper Co. v. Moody* decision, subjective supervisory appraisals of job performance are inherently suspect if they produce adverse impact against a protected group. To stand up to the scrutiny of the courts, these judgments must be considered fair and job-related. Whenever possible, base your appraisals on objective evidence. Ask yourself whether the employee's work has met quantity and quality standards, whether the employee has met relevant deadlines. Quantity is easier to measure objectively than quality, but as the above *EEO Today* article says, "both are on firmer ground than criteria that measure personal characteristics."

4. *Document! Keep records.* That's the only way you can support whatever subjective judgments creep into the appraisal process (they're inevitable). Keep records of past appraisals and all the training materials used to comply with EEO regulations.

Be consistent in the length of time you retain records (see p. 42).

5. *Aim for a group of appraisers who have common demographic characteristics with the group being appraised.* This criterion was established in *Rowe v. General Motors.* When only white males appraise blacks, Hispanics, women, and other protected groups, the courts question the fairness of the system. Once a system is challenged and shown to have adverse impact, the company must prove its validity.

6. *Never directly or indirectly imply that race, color, religion, sex, age, national origin, handicap, or veteran status was a factor in your appraisal decision.* Making any discriminatory statement, orally or in writing, will make your organization subject to court action.

7. *Submit the appraisal to several reviewers, especially if it is negative.* To prevent conscious or unconscious bias from creeping into the appraisal process, develop a multilevel review system. Have your superior review and sign the appraisal. This system of checks and balances will reduce the risk of a losing court action.

WARNING: EEO regulations are changing every day, and it's your responsibility as a manager to keep up with current legal developments. Constant scrutiny is the only way to be sure that your appraisal system remains a viable business tool.

PART 3: The performance appraisal interview

Now that you understand the performance appraisal process and know how to prepare yourself and your employees for the appraisal, you are ready to conduct the interview. Knowing what to do when you sit face to face with the employee is the subject of Part 3.

10. ORGANIZE THE APPRAISAL INTERVIEW

Problem: The Planless Interview

"Laura! Am I glad I bumped into you!" said Mindy Walker as she rode down in the elevator with Laura Daniels, a fellow manager at the Easy Carry Bag Company.

"What's up?" asked Laura.

"You know that performance appraisal interview I had scheduled for today?"

"The one you were nervous about all week?"

"Yeah, that one," answered Mindy with a forced smile. "It fell apart on me. As soon as the interview started, I couldn't tie my thoughts together. I didn't know what I was doing and it showed."

"How did you handle it?" asked Laura. "I mean, what did you say to the employee?"

"After I mumbled something about a forgotten meeting, I told her I would have to continue the appraisal tomorrow. The trouble is I still don't know how I'll handle it. What do you suggest?"

*   *   *   *   *

Step 10: Organize the Appraisal Interview

There's no substitute for preparation. That is especially true for such an emotionally charged situation as a performance appraisal interview. Many different steps occur before, during, and after the interview. These steps are always the same—regardless of the nature of the appraisal.

How to Conduct the Interview

The way you approach the interview—your frame of mind—is critical. You do not sit in judgment; you engage in a constructive dialog that allows employees to evaluate their performances and enables both of you to develop a plan of action to make a good performance better or a bad performance acceptable.

BEFORE THE INTERVIEW

1. *Assemble the data.* Collect all the information you need for the interview. First, review the relevant job analysis or job description. Second, compare the employee's performance against these criteria. Third, look back in the files at the employee's previous performance appraisal. Ask yourself whether the employee has met the goals set. (Be careful not to let these past evaluations influence your impressions of the employee's current performance.) Fourth, request comments from other managers who have observed the employee's work. Finally, complete the appraisal form. It will enable you to conduct an organized interview.

Lopez warns against developing an improvement plan at this point. Hold that for the interview itself and leave the primary responsibility to the employee.

2. *Prepare the employee.* Always give your employees fair warning of when their performance appraisal interviews are to

take place. They should have at least a week's notice to review their work, read over their job description or job analysis, analyze problems, and gather their questions and comments. When you notify your employees of the date for their appraisals, stress that the appraisal is designed mainly to help them know where they stand.

3. *Choose the time and place.* Work out a mutually agreeable time for the interview. Lopez suggests divorcing the interview from troublesome incidents. Plan it for a day when your relationship with your employees is at its best, he advises.

Be sure to allow enough time in your schedule for the entire interview. (Of course, warn your employees to do the same.) You can expect interviews with lower-level personnel (clerical workers, maintenance staff, mailroom employees, etc.) to take no more than an hour. Appraising higher-level personnel (management and professional employees) often takes two or three times longer.

Choose a private place for the interview where you are unlikely to be bothered by phone calls, visitors, and other interruptions. Truell suggests using an office other than your own as a way of encouraging an equal interchange of ideas and feelings. Try to find what Lopez calls a "neutral meeting place"—one without a desk or large conference table to form a barrier between you.

DURING THE INTERVIEW

1. *Set the tone at the start of the interview.* Your aim is to relax your employees. As you tell the employee how the interview will proceed and what you hope to accomplish, define the roles each of you will play. Make clear, says Truell, that you are having a two-way conversation. Emphasize that the employee has your undivided attention and that you have blocked out an extended time period for the appraisal.

2. *Ask the employee to evaluate his or her own performance.* To be sure that your frames of reference are the same, Truell suggests that you ask employees to restate their performance

objectives for the period and analyze how well they have met these objectives.

Use whatever the employee says as a jumping-off point for the interview. An employee who paints an unrealistic picture of past performance should be handled differently from an employee who gives you an honest appraisal. Use this period to understand how your employees view their work. If you have questions or need clarification, ask the employee to repeat any point about which you are unclear. Try to maintain an atmosphere that encourages an honest give-and-take.

3. *Give your assessment of the employee's strong and weak points.* Be as positive as you can in your praise and criticism. Instead of talking about mistakes, faults, or weaknesses, talk about constructive steps the employee can take to do a better job. Try to be descriptive, not evaluative, in presenting the assessment information. For example, talk about an unmet sales quota rather than the employee's poor job performance. And focus on solving problems rather than rehashing past events. (We will talk more about specific techniques for interviewing the effective and ineffective employees in Chapters 11 and 12.)

4. *Summarize your own and your employee's views.* Truell suggests that you talk about strong points and weaknesses of performance and the reasons why the employee should try to improve. Distinguish areas in which you and your employee differ and try to resolve these differences by focusing on your reasons for change. You might convince the employee to try another tack. Often, however, the employee will continue to disagree with you. That's okay. Your aim is a complete *understanding* of each other's views.

5. *Develop an action plan in cooperation with your employee.* Choose goals that are as specific and practical as possible. Then compare them to what the employee has accomplished during the current appraisal period. Remember, you are not *dictating* a plan of action. You are working *with* the employee to develop a viable plan. Lopez suggests focusing on the two or three most important goals instead of all the areas that need improvement.

Then set up a timetable for reaching these goals and devise ways of measuring their achievement. (For specific techniques you can use to improve employee performance, see Chapters fourteen and fifteen.)

As you develop the plan, be aware of problems that may require time to solve or are outside the employee's control. For example, to improve performance, an employee may need additional education, job experience, counseling, greater responsibility, or, as Lopez points out, even a new supervisor.

6. *Conclude the interview.* When you and the employee have covered all points and are satisfied with the improvement plan, the interview is complete. Before expressing thanks for the employee's time and effort, summarize the main points once more. Emphasize the future actions the employee will take to improve performance, and schedule follow-up dates to review the progress. Lopez suggests that you ask the employee to summarize the plan of action, thereby reinforcing the commitment to change. Try to conclude the interview on a positive note.

AFTER THE INTERVIEW

1. *Don't skimp on the follow-up.* Follow-up is the most crucial and the most ignored aspect of the performance appraisal process. It is during the follow-up period that you monitor your employees' progress against the specific goals and timetable established in the interview. It is also the time to play *your* part in improving your employees' work by giving them the training and individual attention they need to reach their goals. You may have to hold monthly progress meetings with your employees and keep records and notes, but in the long run, the results are worth the effort.

Why does the performance appraisal follow-up often fall short? One reason is that many managers tend to think of performance appraisals as one-shot deals: once they conduct the interview they are finished until the next year. Another reason is that the demands of their busy schedules take over and they overlook their employees' needs. Lopez warns that if you ignore the follow-up, your subordinate will likely approach the next performance evaluation interview with skepticism.

2. *Write an appraisal report summarizing the areas of agreement and disagreement and the action plan.* Give a copy to the employee and file a copy as a record of the meeting.

WARNING: Talking about money places you in the position of judging the employee's worth—assigning a dollar sign to the employee's value to the organization. Even though these judgments are part of the appraisal process, they should not cloud the appraisal interview itself: any discussion or expected discussion of money will likely override your performance appraisal and suggestions for improvement.

What to do? Kellogg suggests informing your employees of their pay increases and allowing a brief adjustment period before you schedule the appraisal interview. If employees raise the salary issue at the interview, discuss increases in the context of their work performance.

---

11. AIM THE EFFECTIVE EMPLOYEE TOWARD EXCELLENCE

Problem: The Perfect Employee

"Hey, Tom. What's up? You look a little confused." Andy Gerard's good-natured question brought a smile to Tom Ford's face.

"I should have these problems all the time," said Tom, the sales manager of a furniture manufacturing business. "David Petry's performance appraisal interview is due and I don't know what to say."

"Isn't Petry your top furniture salesman?" asked Andy.

"That's my problem. He's perfect. He brings in the top sales figures every month—even when I assign him a new territory."

"Well, why don't you just tell him he's Mr. Supersalesman," said Andy, "and then go on to some of your problem employees?"

"I'd like to do that. But he's pressuring me for some constructive criticism. He wants to go places in the company and feels my pointers will help."

"It sounds like you've got to come up with something."

"I wish I knew what that something is."

*   *   *   *   *

Step 11: Help Effective Employees Do an Even Better Job

Tom Ford's mistake was to think of David Petry as the "perfect" employee. No one is. Every employee can be helped to do an even better job. Striving toward excellence and mapping out plans to achieve it are your jobs when you appraise the effective employee's performance.

How to Appraise the Effective Employee

1. *Work with the employee to define the present situation and to list ways both you and the employee can improve work performance in the future*. Have effective employees spend most of the interview analyzing where they are now and where they are going.

One way to do this is to use the problem-solving approach discussed in Chapter twelve. Since you are working with an employee who is already doing a good job, point this problem-solving technique toward the goal of excellence. Brainstorm with the employee, suggests Lopez, to come up with a specific course of action. In David Petry's performance appraisal interview, for example, Tom could have helped David think of ways for increasing client sales and generating new clients.

2. *Be an active listener*. Your aim is to counsel the employee, not to judge the person or conduct the interview in an authoritarian manner. The best way to do this, according to Lopez, is to make "it appear as though the employee is inter-

viewing you." Sit back and listen as the employee explains plans for the future. Avoid preaching or cross-examining. Instead, try to work your comments into the flow of the employee's talk. Make them appear to be a natural part of the employee's own thinking.

Dessler breaks this process of active listening into the following steps.

- *Listen for total meaning.* That means hearing your employees' words and their underlying meanings. To be an active listener, says Dessler, you must "get 'inside' the person you are listening to." You must try to understand what your employees think and *feel* about their work.
- *Reflect your employees' feelings.* To help your employees understand what they feel, repeat and summarize their statements. (Sometimes even strong feelings are not part of the employee's consciousness.)
- *Be aware of all verbal and nonverbal cues.* Facial expressions, body language, hesitations in speech, and voice inflections can tell you a lot about your employees' feelings. For example, an individual who hugs his body nervously and stutters during the interview may feel threatened by what you say.
- *Don't be judgmental.* Negative judgments are threats to a person's self-esteem. They get in the way of employees' ability to confront their feelings about their work and to decide on an improvement plan. So stop yourself as you are about to give some "helpful advice" and remember that you may get a lot further by taking a less direct approach.
- *Show your interest.* None of this will work if your employees sense your lack of interest. If you would rather be doing something else than conducting the appraisal, put off the interview until you can give the employee your full attention.

3. *First talk about the weaknesses of your effective employees and then praise their strengths.* Your main objective is to communi-

cate to your employees that they are doing a superior job. If you say this at the beginning of the interview and conclude with a discussion of problems, they will come away with the feeling that you are dissatisfied with their work. According to Lopez, studies have shown that in an interview situation, employees will remember most what is told to them last. So start out with a short discussion of their weaknesses and spend the bulk of the interview reinforcing the employees' good work.

WARNING: If you are thinking of promoting employees, make sure the characteristics that make them assets to you also apply to the new position. Kellogg suggests that managers evaluating employee potential should check employees' educational and work histories to make sure they can handle the work ahead; find out how well employees have applied their experience and education in their present jobs; if possible, use formal, job-related aptitude tests to gauge employees' ability to do the new work; and use the skills of a detective in talking to employees about their past accomplishments and career goals.

---

12. TRY TO HELP THE INEFFECTIVE EMPLOYEE

Problem: A Garbled Message

Michelle Cooper, production manager of Best Toy Company, walked into Marvin Warren's office and closed the door. As she sank into the chair next to his desk, she started grumbling.

"Sometimes I think that everyone is speaking a different language."

"What do you mean?" asked Marvin. "Something must have really gone wrong to ruffle those smooth feathers of yours."

"It was Bert Simon's performance appraisal. Every time I said white, he thought I said black. I spent over an hour with him and accomplished nothing."

"Isn't Bert the guy you've been having a lot of trouble with? The one who's two steps away from being fired?"

"That's right," said Michelle. She thought for a moment before she went on. "Maybe that's why he didn't hear anything I said. It was just too painful for him to listen."

*   *   *   *   *

Step 12: Learn How to Deal With the Ineffective Employee

Michelle Cooper is faced with a problem that often arises when appraising ineffective employees. The situation is so supercharged with emotions for the employees (no one likes to get a bad review) that they misperceive: they unconsciously protect their self-image by denying there is a problem. Michelle's own uneasiness may have made the situation worse. Embarrassed by what she had to say, she may have unintentionally garbled the message. "The sternest test comes," says Lopez, "in coping with the ineffective employee."

Avoiding this kind of miscommunication involves several steps. Start by thinking of the ineffective employee as a special appraisal problem. Then develop the skills you need to deal with the problem.

How to Cope With the Ineffective Employee

1. *Recognize that people respond differently to criticism*. Without this understanding, your interview is doomed before it begins. Lopez suggests that you try to tailor your interview to the following major personality types:

- *The peaceful fighter*. These employees react to criticism by disagreeing with your analysis of their work and by trying to prove that your evaluation is wrong. To handle this kind of response, state your views, but don't press for total agreement. This may take several interviews to accomplish—if it comes at all. Listen to the employees' views, but try to avoid getting involved in a heated debate. Remember, they perceive their positions to be correct. They are unlikely to change their minds on the spot.

  But an employee may convince *you* that your view is unreasonable or incorrect. Try to regard every compromise as a step forward rather than as a point lost. With major sticking points eliminated, the employee may be more willing to listen to you.

- *The surface agree-er.* Some employees will agree with all your criticism without even a mild protest. But, as Lopez points out, agreement is not always the same as acceptance. You may, in fact, have a hollow victory on your hands—a victory that stems from one of the following problems:

  — Inability to understand what you have said and how your rating affects the employee's future in the organization.

  — Employee anxiety. These employees are so anxious about your comments that they will do anything to avoid additional problems.

  — Employee submissiveness. These employees agree with you because they believe it is respectful or polite.

  To find out if surface agreement is a problem, ask employees to rate their performances at the beginning of the interview. If they radically change their positions without any struggle, you have reason to worry.

- *The quitter.* Some employees collapse under the weight of criticism. They would rather resign than try to work out their problems. Embarrassed by their poor performances and by your opinion of them, they offer their resignation on the spot. Even if this is what you wanted, Lopez warns against precipitously accepting such a resignation: it shakes the confidence other employees have in the appraisal process. There is a big difference in every employee's mind between a considered resignation and one directly tied to an unfavorable performance review.

  If an employee offers to resign after the appraisal interview, try to find out why. Then point out the person's strong points and try to show that the resignation was premature.

- *The unresponsive employee.* Occasionally, you may face employees who answer your criticism with one-word replies. To deal with this, says Lopez, you may have to leave your interview plan and try to build a thread of conversation.

  Use open-ended, declarative statements to force these employees to respond. (For example, "I noticed that your sales figures are down this month.") Listen carefully to the employees' answers and encourage them to tell you their job-related problems. The more the employees talk, the more comfortable they will feel and the more likely they will open up further.

- *The buck passer.* These employees try to blame others for their faults. It is your job to make them accept responsibility for their performances, including their failures.

  To do this, accept their admission of even the smallest fault noncommittally. Each time this happens, they will feel more confident in their own ability to deal with your response.

2. *Take a problem-solving approach.* This is the only approach that can succeed, says Lopez. Here are the steps he outlines for dealing with a performance failure:

- *Define the problem.* Analyze the situation with the employee. Try to find out what happened to create the problem and how the employee feels about it. Spend a lot of time listening before you decide what to do.
- *Reflect.* After listening to the employee, consider the possibility of reinterpreting your evaluation. Be sure to question the employee about any hazy areas. Say that you understand the employee's point of view and, to be sure there is no misinterpretation, summarize it.

- *Clarify.* Come to an agreement on what the problem is. State it clearly.
- *Analyze the problem.* Express your feelings about the problem and encourage the employee to work with you to find a solution.
- *Get a commitment.* Get a pledge from the employee to try to change the situation and to work with you in a specific, goal-directed improvement program.
- *Feedback.* Find out if the employee understands and accepts the decisions and has the apparent motivation to carry them through.

3. *Conduct the interview as a consultant, not a judge.* In order to get the most cooperation out of your employees and encourage them to improve their performances, act as a consultant, an advisor, and an information source. It is important to play down your supervisory role, at least at the start, so that your employees feel less threatened by what you are about to say. The anxiety they feel when you judge them gets in the way of meaningful communication.

If you approach these employees as a consultant—someone who informs them of the standards you expect but does not give orders—you are more likely to avoid defensive, angry reactions than if you conduct a disciplinary interview. As Lopez says, you might have to "admonish, warn, and threaten" employees when all else fails, but you should wait until you have no other choice.

4. *Remain calm in the face of the employee's anger.* Try to calm down an employee who explodes in anger. Remain composed and accept some of the responsibility for the poor performance. The employee will feel that you are working on the problem together and that she or he is not out on a limb alone. When the employee is more comfortable with your joint effort, suggest that you work together on finding a solution.

WARNING: Focus on the employee's job *performance* rather than the employee. Nothing makes people more defensive than an attack on their personal characteristics. For example, instead of talking about how sloppy an employee is, focus on her illegible reports and the trouble you have deciphering her work.

13. SPOT PROBLEMS THAT CAN RUIN THE APPRAISAL INTERVIEW

Problem: The Nonreceptive Employee

Albert Simon shook his head as he walked into his office. He had just spent the last two hours talking to Ned Butler about his work—or maybe he should say talking to himself about Ned's work.

"I don't know what to make of it," thought Albert. "Ned is usually so enthusiastic during his appraisal interview. But today he just sat there saying nothing. He didn't seem to care what I said either way. I wonder if anything is wrong."

*   *   *   *   *

Step 13: Analyze the Source of the Problem

A lot may be wrong. Any of a variety of factors can get in the way of an effective performance appraisal interview. Try to head off these problems before the interview so that your employee benefits fully from the appraisal process.

How to Spot Problems That Can Ruin the Appraisal Interview

1. *Keep your eye out for factors that might affect your employees' response to the interview.* Uncovering these factors is not easy. It requires a questioning approach and an understanding of human motivation. Kellogg advises managers to be aware of the following factors:

- *Personal problems.* Health, family, and financial problems can sidetrack even the superstars. When employees are dealing with these kinds of concerns, they often have little tolerance for a discussion of their job performance. If possible, wait for the crisis to end before you go ahead with the appraisal.
- *Unusual work pressures.* If your employees feel harried by the demands placed on their time or if they are in the middle of learning a new operational system or trying to solve a complex technical problem, they will not be receptive to the appraisal interview. Taking two or three hours out of their day will only make them more anxious about their work. Try to wait until the next slack period before you raise the appraisal issue.
- *How the employee feels about you.* An employee engaged in bitter rivalry with you is not likely to be interested in your appraisal remarks. This kind of rivalry is likely to develop, says Kellogg, between an employee who wanted the position of manager and the indi-

vidual chosen for the position. Similarly, employees may turn off a manager who is considerably younger than they are or who has less experience. In both cases, give your employees as much time as possible to get used to you. And give yourself the chance to prove your work to the employee.

- *Desire for advancement.* The itch to move up is a powerful incentive, and employees who see a place for themselves in the organization will be receptive to your comments. When employees are in a dead-end job, however, they probably will pay little attention to what you say. Try to encourage these employees to open themselves up to new ways of looking at their work and new challenges.

- *How long since the last raise.* If your employees have gone a long time without a raise or if they were dissatisfied with the amount of the raise, they will approach the interview in a negative frame of mind. As we discussed earlier, always let the employee digest the news of a pay increase before you conduct the appraisal interview.

- *A change in the way you treat the employee.* If suddenly, without explanation, you become more demanding and less responsive to your employees, they may turn off when you begin talking about their performance appraisals. Dealing with this problem usually involves self-appraisal. Analyze why you have changed your attitudes and if these changes are really necessary.

- *No follow-up of other appraisal interviews.* Don't blame your employees for lack of spirit if you have never followed up their previous appraisal interviews. Start now to think of the appraisal interview as an ongoing process that lasts throughout the year.

2. *Try to find out how your employees feel about the interview.* Kellogg suggests these steps:

- Throw out a small suggestion and see how they react.

- Ask your employees how they feel. Find out if they are willing to accept your suggestions and act on them.
- Wait for your employees to make the first move. If your deadline is loose, ask your employees to let you know when they are ready for the appraisal.
- Use the past as your guide. If you are not sure how your employees will act, think back to their previous appraisals. The way they responded then may give you a clue to their behavior now.

WARNING: What your employees think of your managerial skill has a lot to do with how favorably they respond to the appraisal interview. The employee's lack of respect for the manager can undermine the appraisal process in the following examples of employee-manager relationships cited by Kellogg: the feared but respected manager; "the nice guy," the slightly incompetent manager; the over-the-hill manager; the incompetent, disliked manager.

Take a long, hard look at yourself to find out whether you fit into any of these categories. Then begin working on yourself to change the kind of role you play in your employees' work lives.

PART 4: The ongoing appraisal

It's not enough to sit back and watch your employees respond to the sound advice you've given them in the performance appraisal interview. You have to get into the act.

Kellogg calls you a coach. Others define your role as a counselor. Whatever the label, the purpose is the same. You must help develop an action program to improve your employees' performances.

14. COACH
EMPLOYEES

Problem: Progress Report—No Progress

Mike Jones, marketing manager of a car rental company, nervously walked into his boss's office. His boss had sounded angry over the phone.

"I received this marketing report from Stuart Hart this morning," said Mike's boss, "and it's a mess. Figures are missing, facts are out of place. It's useless. This kind of work can't go on. You have to get to Hart right away and get this problem solved."

"I've tried," said Mike. "During Hart's performance appraisal three months ago, I hammered away at his sloppiness—at the way he lets details slide by. He promised to change."

"What have you done since then to keep on top of this?"

"We . . . Well," stuttered Mike. "I expected Hart to take the ball and go with it."

"You mean you dropped the issue after Hart's review?"

"I didn't have time," answered Mike. "Besides, I did *my* job."

"Only part of it," snapped his boss. "You forgot the part that could have made the difference."

*   *   *   *   *

Step 14: Use a Coaching Appraisal

Mike made two serious mistakes that all but guaranteed a performance appraisal with no results. First, he thought of the appraisal as a one-shot affair that rode on the success or failure of the interview itself. And second, he never considered his role in improving Hart's performance.

Kellogg believes the manager plays a crucial role in changing employee work habits. She advises managers to approach the performance appraisal as a coach whose role is to help employees learn. The following draws on Kellogg's suggested steps for turning a performance appraisal into a coaching appraisal.

How to Coach Employees

1. *Relate information gathered on the employee's past performance to the work that lies ahead.* Determine how closely your employees' proven abilities match the kind of work you anticipate for them in the next six to twelve months. (Consult Chapter 2 for the most effective ways to observe your employees' performances.)

2. *List all the major work assignments you expect the employee to undertake in the coming months.* You can do this by brainstorming your own goals, by analyzing the employee's job description or job analysis, or by consulting the overall department plan. Make each item on the list as specific as possible. Mention all the products, people, companies, and so on, that will be involved in

the upcoming jobs. This will help plan the employee's goals and give you a way of measuring the employee's success later.

3. *Analyze how well the employee has been able to complete similar jobs in the past.* Try not to overgeneralize or to use only recent information. To get a more balanced view, check past performance appraisal forms (especially those that list critical incidents), and in the case of new employees, personnel records and preemployment information. You can also check with former managers or ask the employee for a self-appraisal analyzing strong and weak points. Always remember your goal throughout this process is to compare the employee's past accomplishments against future work assignments.

4. *Try to anticipate future events that might affect the employee's ability to do the job.* What are the situational factors that can turn your employee's work environment upside down? These include changes within the company (Are any major product, organizational, or personnel changes being planned?), outside the company in the immediate business environment (Is your product line being threatened by new competition or technology? Are customer buying habits changing?) and in the political and economic environment (Are new tax laws being passed? Are new government regulations being formulated?). Try to gauge how each of these anticipated events will affect the employee's ability to do the job.

5. *List the ways you can help the employee do a better job.* Ask yourself what you can do to help the employee reach future goals. Then list these ways next to each anticipated work assignment.

By passing on your knowledge and experience, clarifying the work assignments and expected results, steering the employees away from expected obstacles, giving employees the help they need to develop new skills, discussing options, and reviewing their progress, you will help move your employees toward their desired goals. You can add to this joint effort by setting up contacts and leads, providing additional resources, identifying sources of help, making needed organizational changes, and so on.

6. *Ask your employees to suggest ways you can help.* Your

employees know their needs better than anyone else. Take advantage of this by asking them to suggest things you can do.

7. *Set priorities for you and your employees*. Choose the areas that employees should concentrate on, select the best methods for employees to improve their performances, and pinpoint the specific ways you can help.

8. *Write your conclusions down*. Putting your coaching appraisal into writing helps commit you to carrying it through.

WARNING: Avoid giving employees the feeling that improvement is solely their responsibility. As Bittel points out, "improvement is almost always a mutually dependent activity." When employees know this, they are bound to approach their work with greater confidence and enthusiasm.

15. DEVELOP A LEARNING PLAN

Problem: No Goals

"I don't know what Mr. Perkins wants from me," said Anita Turner, production coordinator at a medium-sized jewelry manufacturing company, to Rick Sherman, the design coordinator. "Just this morning he told me he's not happy with my work, but he never tells me what's bothering him."

"Didn't he lay that out in your performance appraisal? You know—what your strong points are and where you need improvement. When my boss and I discussed my work, we even put together an improvement plan."

"I wish Mr. Perkins had done that. Right now the only .hing he's doing is driving me crazy with his complaints."

* * * * *

Step 15: Develop a Learning Plan

The only way a performance appraisal can work is if you develop a plan of action aimed at helping employees improve their performances. In short, you have to set up the conditions that enable employees to learn. We referred to this plan in Chapter 10. We will now break it down into the specific learning steps suggested by Kellogg.

How to Guide the Employee Through the Learning Process

1. *Set specific goals.* Translate the desired improvement into learning goals. Stick to only one or two goals at a time so your employees can put their complete effort into reaching them. Try to make the goals specific and measurable. This will help your employees target what they must do. It will also allow them—and you—to know when they have achieved success. Be sure that the improved performance you seek is for the employee's normal job duties.

2. *Motivate your employees to commit themselves to reaching these goals.* You cannot do the work for your employees, so this commitment is extremely important.

3. *Give your employees the resources they need to reach their goals.* Information, tools, staff support are all essential ingredients for improved performance. You must provide this support for your employees or give them the opportunity to find it themselves.

4. *Allow the employee to apply the information.* Learning is tied to doing. You must provide your employees with repeated opportunities to apply and refine new skills.

5. *Provide regular feedback.* At every reasonable opportunity, tell your employees how they are doing and offer them private, constructive criticism. Public praise is a powerful motivating tool, so don't forget to use it whenever the opportunity arises.

6. *Persevere until your employees have reached their goals.*

7. *Reward successful efforts through pay increases, promotions, and other incentives.* Reward is an important part of the learning process. It makes employees feel that their efforts have paid off.

WARNING: Guiding the employee through the learning process requires a close working relationship based on mutual respect and interest. So before you begin directing your energy toward improved performance, spend some time building solid working ties. They will pay off with dividends later.

CONCLUSION

Saul W. Gellerman, author of *The Management of Human Resources*, reflects the views of many personnel experts concerning the current state of performance appraisals. "Few, if any, aspects of management," says Gellerman, "reveal as disappointing a gap between potential and actuality as does performance appraisal." Instead of contributing to improved employee performance, better morale, increased managerial effectiveness and overall personnel practices, it often accomplishes little—a fact that is unfortunate but true.

It is within *your* power to transform performance appraisal into a truly workable system—one that gives you, the employee, and the organization valuable information unavailable elsewhere and that motivates employees to higher standards of performance.

Bringing about this change requires a commitment to the attitudes, knowledge, and skills we have discussed. Perhaps most of all, it takes an understanding that performance appraisals guide your own actions as well as your employees': what *you* do can mean the difference between success and failure.

Bibliography

Ashe, Jr., R. Lawrence. "How Do Your Performance Appraisals Perform?" *EEO Today*, Vol. 7, No. 3, Autumn 1980, pp. 216–22.

Bigoness, William J. "Effects of Applicants' Sex, Race, and Performance on Employer's Performance Rating: Some Additional Findings." *Journal of Applied Psychology*, Vol. 61, No. 1, February 1976.

Bittel, Lester R. *What Every Supervisor Should Know.* 3rd ed. N.Y.: McGraw-Hill Book Co., 1974, pp. 195–208.

Cummings, L. L. and Schwab, Donald P. *Performance in Organizations: Determinants and Appraisals.* Glenview, Ill.: Scott, Foresman and Co., 1973.

Dessler, Gary. *Management Fundamentals: A Framework.* 2nd ed. Reston, Va.: Reston Publishing Co., 1979, pp. 241–72.

Finn, Robert H. "Is Your Appraisal Program Really Necessary?" *Personnel*, Vol. 37, January–February 1960, pp. 16–25.

Gellerman, Saul W. *The Management of Human Resources.* Hinsdale, Ill.: The Dryden Press, 1976, pp. 165–80.

Glueck, William F. *Foundations of Personnel.* Dallas: Business Publications, Inc., 1979, pp. 198–233.

Keil, E. C. *Performance Appraisals and the Manager.* N.Y.: Lebhar-Friedman Books, 1977.

Kellogg, Marion S. *What to Do About Performance Appraisals.* N.Y.: AMACOM, 1975.

Kirchner, W. K. and Dunnette, M. D. "Identifying the Critical Factors in Successful Salesmanship." *Personnel*, Vol. 34, 1957, pp. 54–59.

Lazer, Robert I. and Wikstrom, Walter S. *Appraising Managerial Performance: Current Practices and Future Directions.* N.Y.: The Conference Board, 1977.

Lopez, Felix M. *Personnel Interviewing: Theory and Practice.* 2nd ed. N.Y.: McGraw-Hill Book Co., 1975, pp. 200–44.

"Performance Appraisals: The Next EEO Frontier?" *EEO Today*, Vol. 4, No. 3, Autumn 1977, pp. 149–58.

"Reducing the EEO Risks in Performance Appraisals." *EEO Today*, Vol. 7, No. 3, Autumn 1980, pp. 161–68.

Truell, George F. *Performance Appraisal: Current Issues & New Directions.* Buffalo, N.Y.: PAT Publications, 1980.